ATTILA THE HUN

WAS KILLED BY A NOSEBLEED

And Other Facts About History

TRUE OR FALSE?

ATTILA THE HUN

WAS KILLED BY A NOSEBLEED

And Other Facts About History

JAN PAYNE AND STEVEN WILDER

Enslow Publishing
101 W. 23rd Street
Suite 240
New York, NY 10011
USA
enslow.com

Published in 2017 by Enslow Publishing, LLC.
101 W. 23rd Street, Suite 240, New York, NY 10011

Published in 2017 by Enslow Publishing, LLC, by permission of the Reader's Digest Association Inc., 44 South Broadway, White Plains, New York, 10601.

Library of Congress Cataloging-in-Publication Data
Names: Payne, Jan. | Wilder, Steven.
Title: Attila the Hun was killed by a nosebleed : and other facts about history / Jan Payne and Steven Wilder.
Description: New York, NY : Enslow Publishing, 2017. | Series: True or false? | Audience: Ages 8 and up. | Includes bibliographical references and   index.
Identifiers: LCCN 2016005252| ISBN 9780766077263 (library bound) | ISBN 9780766077249 (paperback) | ISBN 9780766077256 (6-pack)
Subjects: LCSH: History--Miscellanea--Juvenile literature. | Curiosities and wonders--Juvenile literature.
Classification: LCC D10 .P39 2017 | DDC 909--dc23
LC record available at http://lccn.loc.gov/2016005252

Printed in the United States of America

To Our Readers: We have done our best to make sure all website addresses in this book were active and appropriate when we went to press. However, the author and the publisher have no control over and assume no liability for the material available on those websites or on any websites they may link to. Any comments or suggestions can be sent by e-mail to customerservice@enslow.com.

Cover art by Joel R. Gennari

Interior illustrations by Paul Moran

Photo credits: maodoltee/Shutterstock.com (backgrounds throughout book); Nobelus/Shutterstock. com (dingbat on spine).

CONTENTS

Introduction

Did you know that Genghis Kahn had molten silver poured into the eyes and ears of a defeated enemy? That Ancient Egyptians mummified their dead to keep them from smelling? Or did they? This book is full of fascinating facts and fat fibs—and it's up to you to decipher which is which.

From facts about historical figures, events, and even creatures, you will have a great time testing your knowledge, while learning some astonishing truths and uncovering some large lies along the way. Then check out the shocking facts that follow to see if your lie-detecting skills are up to snuff.

IT'S UP TO YOU

Here's how it works. Each section contains a list of facts. On a separate sheet of paper, write down which you think really happened and which are big fat fibs.

There's a chart on page 41 that you can copy to help you keep your score for each section. Then find out your grand total by adding up how many of these facts you got right!

So what are you waiting for? Grab a pencil and see if you can spot the twisted truths. Why not test your family and friends to see if they know the facts? You never know! You may surprise them with some of the stranger-than-fiction truths waiting to amaze you on these fun-packed pages.

Chapter One

DELIGHTFUL DINOS

QUIZ Dinosaurs ruled the Earth for 185 million years, but how long will it take you to spot the mistruths about these amazing animals? Mark your answers on another piece of paper, and find out if you're a dino expert.

THE "FACTS"

	TRUE	FALSE
1. The T-Rex was the fastest dinosaur.	☐	☐
2. The Nigersaurus was used as a vacuum cleaner by other dinosaurs.	☐	☐
3. The Pterodactyl was a flying reptile.	☐	☐
4. The name "dinosaur" comes from the verb "to dine" or "to eat" because dinosaurs ate constantly.	☐	☐
5. The smallest dinosaurs were no bigger than chickens.	☐	☐
6. Dinosaurs grew so large because the prey they ate was huge, too.	☐	☐
7. Dinosaurs died out because the big ones ate all the little ones and then starved to death because they had nothing left to eat.	☐	☐

1. THE T-REX WAS THE FASTEST DINOSAUR.

FALSE

The T-Rex could run at speeds of only 15 miles (24 km) per hour, less than half as fast as the Gallimimus, a fast-moving birdlike dinosaur that could move at speeds of up to 35 miles (56 km) per hour.

2. THE NIGERSAURUS WAS USED AS A VACUUM CLEANER BY OTHER DINOSAURS.

FALSE

The Nigersaurus did have a mouth that looked and worked exactly like a vacuum cleaner, but it didn't do any cleaning. This delightful dinosaur had wide lips and over 500 tiny teeth that it used to chomp really close to the ground and suck up grass and ferns. When it wore down its teeth with the constant chomping, other teeth, which were stashed in rows behind the front teeth, took over. The Nigersaurus had a very long neck, so it could mow down loads of plants while standing in one spot.

3. THE PTERODACTYL WAS A FLYING REPTILE.

TRUE

These high-flyers were winged reptiles, related to dinosaurs. Their arms were modified into wings, with a leathery web connecting the tip of the fourth finger—which was 10 times longer than the other fingers—to the foot.

4. THE NAME "DINOSAUR" COMES FROM THE VERB "TO DINE" OR "TO EAT," BECAUSE DINOSAURS ATE CONSTANTLY.

FALSE

The name "dinosaur" comes from two Greek words that mean "terrible lizard." In fact, dinosaurs were not lizards, and only a few were terrible. Most dinosaurs were about as fierce as cows and spent their time munching on leafy greens.

5. THE SMALLEST DINOSAURS WERE NO BIGGER THAN CHICKENS.

TRUE

The smallest dinosaur was the Compsognathus, which was the same size as a chicken. It walked on two long, thin legs and had two short arms with clawed fingers on each hand. It could run fast and ate insects and lizards.

6. DINOSAURS GREW SO LARGE BECAUSE THE PREY THEY ATE WAS HUGE, TOO.

FALSE

Many of the largest dinosaurs, such as the Brontosaurus, which grew up to 90 feet (27 m) long, were actually plant eaters. They were so huge because the plants they ate were really tough to digest. The dinos' teeth weren't very good at chewing, so their stomachs had to break down the food instead. To do this, they needed to be huge, rumbling digestion tanks—and big stomachs needed to be carried in big bodies!

7. DINOSAURS DIED OUT BECAUSE THE BIG ONES ATE ALL THE LITTLE ONES AND THEN STARVED TO DEATH BECAUSE THEY HAD NOTHING LEFT TO EAT.

FALSE

Scientists have many ideas about why dinosaurs died out, or became extinct, but this isn't one of them. The most popular idea is that a giant meteorite hit the Earth, throwing up a huge dust cloud. This would have quickly changed the entire world's climate for a long time, perhaps killing the dinosaurs. Of course, no one knows what happened for sure, but scientists are learning more all the time.

AMAZING ANCIENTS

QUIZ

Centuries ago, during ancient times, some pretty amazing things took place. Some of them were advanced, while others seem very odd today. But which are real and which are fake? Mark your choices on a separate piece of paper, and check your answers to find out if you're an ancient history authority!

THE "FACTS"

	TRUE	FALSE
1. Like the Egyptians, the Aztecs built pyramids to use as royal tombs.	☐	☐
2. The Romans had an amazingly advanced plumbing system.	☐	☐
3. Ancient Greece was the first country to hold the Olympic Games.	☐	☐
4. The Egyptians mummified their dead to stop them from smelling.	☐	☐
5. The Phoenicians were the first people to record things by writing them down.	☐	☐
6. The first farmland in ancient Britain was called the Fertile Crescent.	☐	☐

1. LIKE THE EGYPTIANS, THE AZTECS BUILT PYRAMIDS TO USE AS ROYAL TOMBS.

FALSE

The Aztecs lived in what is now Mexico. Their civilization flourished until the arrival of Spanish conquerors, known as the conquistadors, in the 16th century. While it is true that, like the Egyptians, the Aztecs built huge, pyramid-like, stepped structures known as ziggurats, these were not tombs. They towered above the buildings below them, and their steps led to flat tops, on which temples stood. These temples were used in the worship of the Aztec gods. Priests offered human sacrifices to the gods, ripping the heart from the victim's chest.

2. THE ROMANS HAD AN AMAZINGLY ADVANCED PLUMBING SYSTEM.

TRUE

The Romans liked to keep clean, and bathing was a sociable pastime. Roman cities had public baths where people would bathe together. The baths were made possible by the Romans' amazing plumbing system. Clean, fresh water was carried into towns and cities from streams via aqueducts—bridges or tunnels that channelled the water at a steady pace from its source. At the baths the water flowed in through lead pipes. Some rooms were also heated with an under-floor heating system, and sewers carried waste away, dumping it into rivers. After the Roman Empire declined, people returned to their previous filthy ways. Many centuries passed before plumbing became popular once again.

3. ANCIENT GREECE WAS THE FIRST COUNTRY TO HOLD THE OLYMPIC GAMES.

TRUE

The first recorded Olympic Games were held in 776 BC with just one event—a running race. The Games were then held every four years with other events, such as wrestling and chariot racing, added later. The Roman emperor Theodosius I abolished them around 400 AD. The next Games were held almost 1,500 years later, in 1896.

4. THE EGYPTIANS MUMMIFIED THEIR DEAD TO STOP THEM FROM SMELLING.

FALSE

The Egyptians believed that when people died, they lived again in the afterlife. To do this, they needed their body, so it was mummified, or preserved, then laid to rest in a burial chamber inside a tomb. Some kings and queens built huge pyramids to be buried in. As well as the body, the structures housed everything the person would need in the afterlife—from furniture to food and drink.

5. THE PHOENICIANS WERE THE FIRST PEOPLE TO RECORD THINGS BY WRITING THEM DOWN.

FALSE

Many ancient civilizations used early forms of writing to keep records. They were useful to keep track of practical things, such as the crops they were growing. The Sumerians were using symbols to represent letters as early as 3,000 BC. Their form of writing is known as cuneiform. Ancient Egyptians used hieroglyphics—picture symbols standing for words and sounds. The Phoenicians were the first to use a system of writing that is similar to our own, with sounds being represented by symbols and different symbols being combined to make words. This writing was the basis of the alphabet we use today.

6. THE FIRST FARMLAND IN ANCIENT BRITAIN WAS CALLED THE FERTILE CRESCENT.

FALSE

The Fertile Crescent is a region now made up of Iraq, Syria, Lebanon, and Israel. Scientists believe that it was the first place in the world where crops were cultivated. After the Ice Age it had a warm, wet climate with fertile soil, so crops grew well. Two rivers, the Euphrates and the Tigris, were close by, so crops could also be watered. The first farmers grew crops from the seeds collected from wild grain, as well as fruits and vegetables. They also raised animals. Gradually, farming spread through Europe and Asia, and civilizations began to flourish.

Chapter Three

HEROES AND HEROINES

QUIZ

History is chock-full of daring heroes and brave heroines, but can you tell which of the statements below are heroic facts? Mark your answers on a separate sheet of paper to discover if you're a historic hotshot or not!

THE "FACTS"

	TRUE	FALSE
1. Florence Nightingale was known as the Lady with the Lamp because she brought light to thousands of people.	☐	☐
2. Susan B. Anthony was arrested for voting in an election when women couldn't vote.	☐	☐
3. Mahatma Gandhi helped an entire nation gain independence through peace.	☐	☐
4. George Washington seriously considered an offer to become king of the United States.	☐	☐
5. Marie Curie is the only woman who's been awarded two Nobel Prizes.	☐	☐
6. Harriet Tubman helped hundreds of slaves escape via the Underground Railroad.	☐	☐
7. An unidentified American serviceman from World War I is buried in the Tomb of the Unknowns.	☐	☐

1. FLORENCE NIGHTINGALE WAS KNOWN AS THE LADY WITH THE LAMP BECAUSE SHE BROUGHT LIGHT TO THOUSANDS OF PEOPLE.

FALSE

In 1854 Florence Nightingale was an English nurse who was asked to go to a military hospital in Scutari, Turkey, during the Crimean War. Conditions at the hospital were shocking—overcrowded and dirty. Most of the soldiers there were dying from disease rather than as a result of their wounds. Florence worked tirelessly to improve conditions and often walked the hospital at night, with her lamp in hand, checking on her patients. This is how she came to be called the Lady of the Lamp. Florence Nightingale made nursing a respected profession, and many of today's modern practices are based on her thoughts and ideas.

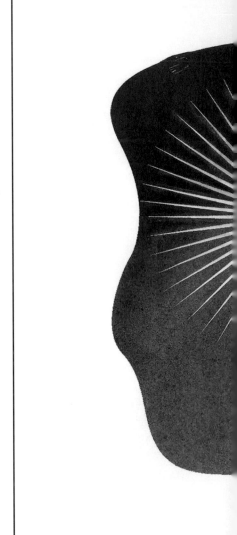

2. SUSAN B. ANTHONY WAS ARRESTED FOR VOTING IN AN ELECTION WHEN WOMEN COULDN'T VOTE.

TRUE

Susan B. Anthony, who fought for the rights of women—including the right to vote—was arrested on November 18, 1872, because she voted in the 1872 presidential election at a time when women were not allowed to vote. She was tried and convicted seven months later and ordered to pay a $100 fine. She refused to pay the fine and continued fighting for women's suffrage. She died fourteen years before the 19th amendment (also known as the Susan B. Anthony amendment) was passed in 1920, giving women the right to vote.

3. MAHATMA GANDHI HELPED AN ENTIRE NATION GAIN INDEPENDENCE THROUGH PEACE.

TRUE

Mohandas Gandhi is often known as Mahatma, which means "great soul." He was an inspirational man who brought about social and political change in India and greatly helped the poor. He inspired fellow Indians to use peaceful protest to try to gain independence from Britain. Gandhi also tried to stop Hindus and Muslims from fighting each other, but in 1948 he was murdered.

4. GEORGE WASHINGTON SERIOUSLY CONSIDERED AN OFFER TO BECOME KING OF THE UNITED STATES.

FALSE

Although Lewis Nicola, a colonel in the Continental army, wrote Washington a letter in 1782 suggesting that Washington consider becoming a king in the new government, Washington was offended by the idea and immediately rejected it. He believed in civilian rule and completely supported the Declaration of Independence. Nicola apologized to Washington several times for bringing up the idea.

5. MARIE CURIE IS THE ONLY WOMAN WHO'S BEEN AWARDED TWO NOBEL PRIZES.

TRUE

Marie Curie was a scientist whose research into radioactivity led to the use of X-rays in medicine. She was awarded the Nobel Prize for Physics in 1903 and for Chemistry in 1911. She is the only woman to have been awarded the Nobel Prize twice.

6. HARRIET TUBMAN HELPED HUNDREDS OF SLAVES ESCAPE VIA THE UNDERGROUND RAILROAD.

TRUE

The Underground Railroad was a network of people who helped slaves escape to freedom. From 1810 to 1850, more than 100,000 southern slaves escaped using this network. When one slave, Harriet Tubman, ran away from her plantation owner in 1849, she fled to the North, where slavery was banned. But Harriet risked her life on 19 occasions, returning south to help more than 300 slaves. She was known to many as Moses because, like Moses in the Bible, she guided slaves to freedom.

7. AN UNIDENTIFIED AMERICAN SERVICEMAN FROM WORLD WAR I IS BURIED IN THE TOMB OF THE UNKNOWNS.

TRUE

On November 11, 1921, this serviceman was buried in the new tomb at Arlington National Cemetery. Later, unidentified servicemen from World War II, the Korean War, and the Vietnam War were buried at the Tomb of the Unknowns, which is also known as the Tomb of the Unknown Soldier (even though it has never been officially named).

Chapter Four

MAD, BAD, AND DANGEROUS TO KNOW

QUIZ

You may have heard of some real-life superheroes, but there have also been some folks throughout history that you definitely wouldn't want to meet! See if you can spot the falsehoods about these shady characters. Keep track of your answers on a separate sheet of paper.

THE "FACTS"

	TRUE	FALSE
1. Genghis Khan had molten silver poured into the eyes and ears of an enemy.	☐	☐
2. Ivan IV of Russia was known as Ivan the Terrible.	☐	☐
3. Al Capone was finally brought to trial, on charges of tax evasion.	☐	☐
4. A Hungarian countess bathed in the blood of young girls to keep her skin youthful.	☐	☐
5. Jack the Ripper was a murderer who was hanged for his crimes in 1888.	☐	☐
6. Attila the Hun, a ferocious warrior, was finished off by a nosebleed.	☐	☐

1. GENGHIS KHAN HAD MOLTEN SILVER POURED INTO THE EYES AND EARS OF AN ENEMY.

TRUE

Genghis Khan was a mighty leader who built the biggest empire in the world during the 12th century. He was ruthless with his enemies. When Genghis Khan captured Inalchuq, a governor of an enemy state, he used this gruesome method to kill him.

2. IVAN IV OF RUSSIA WAS KNOWN AS IVAN THE TERRIBLE.

TRUE

Ivan IV was the first tsar of Russia. He was known as Ivan the Terrible because he was incredibly cruel. He created a huge Russian empire in the 16th century but ruled his people with an iron fist. His wild temper led to him to beating his own son to death in a moment of uncontrollable rage.

3. AL CAPONE WAS FINALLY BROUGHT TO TRIAL, ON CHARGES OF TAX EVASION.

TRUE

From the early 1920s to 1931, Al Capone ran a gang in Chicago that was involved in gambling, smuggling liquor, and other illegal activities. He was the mastermind behind the St. Valentine's Day Massacre, when seven men were killed, and was reputed to have ordered hundreds of murders. Yet Capone wasn't convicted of any of these crimes; instead, he was eventually convicted of income-tax evasion and sent to jail.

4. A HUNGARIAN COUNTESS BATHED IN THE BLOOD OF YOUNG GIRLS TO KEEP HER SKIN YOUTHFUL.

FALSE

Countess Elizabeth Bathory of Hungary is said to have been very cruel, but no one can say for certain if the rumour that she bathed in the blood of young girls is true. According to accounts from witnesses at that time, she did kidnap and torture hundreds of girls with the help of her servants, until her vile crimes were discovered. During a raid on her castle in 1609, men reported that they found many girls dead or dying and others held in cells, awaiting beatings or worse. Bathory was imprisoned in her family castle for the rest of her life.

5. JACK THE RIPPER WAS A MURDERER WHO WAS HANGED FOR HIS CRIMES IN 1888.

FALSE

Jack the Ripper was the nickname of a murderer who stalked the streets of London. He brutally killed five women but was never caught. His identity remains a mystery to this day. He was given his nickname after the police received a letter supposedly written by the murderer and signed, "Jack the Ripper." Many books have been written on the subject of the man who literally got away with murder. In 1892, a convicted serial murder named Thomas Cream did say "I am Jack" right before he was hanged at Newgate prison in London, but few historians think that Thomas Cream was the real Jack the Ripper. But Jack the Ripper's true identity may never be known.

6. ATTILA THE HUN, A FEROCIOUS WARRIOR, WAS FINISHED OFF BY A NOSEBLEED.

TRUE

Attila the Hun was a fearsome warrior and ruler, renowned for his vicious treatment of his enemies. Ironically, in spite of his terrifying reputation, he wasn't killed in battle. He reportedly died at his own wedding in 453 AD. It is said that he had too much to drink, passed out, and choked to death on blood that spewed from a nosebleed.

Chapter Five

WOULD YOU BELIEVE IT?

QUIZ

Humans have accomplished some amazing things. We have also accomplished some things that are just downright strange. See if you can spot the facts from the falsehoods. Keep score on a separate piece of paper & discover if you're a lie detector or just a fib believer.

THE "FACTS"

	TRUE	FALSE
1. The world's hottest chili pepper is 10 times hotter than Tabasco Sauce.	☐	☐
2. In 1957 an April Fool's joke convinced people that spaghetti grows on trees.	☐	☐
3. In Oregon, competitors race around a lake in giant pumpkins.	☐	☐
4. Competitors in extreme ironing have to iron as much as they can in a day.	☐	☐
5. Octopush is an underwater hockey game.	☐	☐
6. The original name for the Google search engine was BackRub.	☐	☐
7. In the 18th century, birds nested in women's elaborate hairstyles.	☐	☐
8. During World War II the government began setting fashion requirements so there was enough fabric available to make parachutes and uniforms.	☐	☐
9. The shortest war in history lasted just 38 minutes.	☐	☐

1. THE WORLD'S HOTTEST CHILI PEPPER IS 10 TIMES HOTTER THAN TABASCO SAUCE.

FALSE

A pepper's chili fire is measured using the Scoville Heat Unit, or SHU. The Infinity chili pepper is a whopping 235 times hotter than tabasco sauce. Tabasco Sauce has a SHU of around 5,000, whereas the Infinity chili scores 1,176,182. Now that's hot!

2. IN 1957 AN APRIL FOOL'S JOKE CONVINCED PEOPLE THAT SPAGHETTI GROWS ON TREES

TRUE

Back in 1957, spaghetti wasn't as widely eaten as it is today. On TV a spoof documentary was broadcast in the UK showing women "harvesting" spaghetti that was draped on the branches of trees. Some people watching the show were so eager to grow their own spaghetti that they called the TV station to find out where they could buy spaghetti trees!

3. IN OREGON, COMPETITORS RACE AROUND A LAKE IN GIANT PUMPKINS.

TRUE

Every October on Lake Tualatin, Oregon, the Giant Pumpkin Regatta is held. There are four races, but before they start, competitors must grab a pumpkin and hollow it out. They then sit in it and float away, paddling around a lake. Ideally, the giant pumpkins should weigh between 600 and 800 pounds (272 and 363 kg). Bigger pumpkins tend to be too slow, but 2010's winner weighed a mighty 1,200 pounds (544 kg).

4. COMPETITORS IN EXTREME IRONING HAVE TO IRON AS MUCH AS THEY CAN IN A DAY.

FALSE

The truth is even stranger. Extreme ironing is one of the craziest "sports" around. It started when two mountaineers set a record for ironing at the highest-ever altitude, on a Swiss mountain. Since then, people have done it while they ski, canoe, or scuba dive. The only rules are that the garment must be at least the size of a dish towel, the iron real, and the board over 3.2 feet (1 m) long.

5. OCTOPUSH IS AN UNDERWATER HOCKEY GAME.

TRUE

This fast and furious underwater sport takes place at the bottom of a swimming pool. Teams play with small handheld sticks that they use to push a puck into the opposing team's goal. The athletes wear a mask, fins, and snorkel, and action happens in brief spurts, between swimming to the surface for air.

6. THE ORIGINAL NAME FOR THE GOOGLE SEARCH ENGINE WAS BACKRUB.

TRUE

In 1996, founders Larry Page and Sergey Brin began the search engine but after a year decided it needed a new name. They came up with Google, playing on the word "googol," a mathematical term that represents the numeral 1 followed by 100 zeros. The use of the term reflects their mission to systemize an infinite amount of information on the Web.

7. IN THE 18TH CENTURY, BIRDS NESTED IN WOMEN'S ELABORATE HAIRSTYLES.

FALSE

In the 18th century it was fashionable to wear huge, elaborate wigs or hairpieces. Some rich people had these wigs built around wire frames, finished off with incredible decorations. The craze was led by Marie Antoinette, the queen of France, whose wig designs even included a model ship! The horsehair and powder that the wigs, or "poufs," were made of were ideal homes for pests such as lice and fleas, so it's likely that they made themselves right at home, even if there were no birds!

8. DURING WORLD WAR II THE GOVERNMENT BEGAN SETTING FASHION REQUIREMENTS SO THERE WAS ENOUGH FABRIC AVAILABLE TO MAKE PARACHUTES AND UNIFORMS.

TRUE

In order to save materials such as wool and silk, which was used for making uniforms and parachutes, first the British and later the American governments passed bills limiting fabric usage. For example, a man's pants could not have pleats or cuffs, and the only colors they came in were black, brown, or navy. The double-breasted coat style was banned, collar widths were slimmed down, the number of pockets was limited, and skirts could not be made from more than two and a half yards of fabric.

9. THE SHORTEST WAR IN HISTORY LASTED JUST 38 MINUTES.

TRUE

The Anglo-Zanzibar War took place on August 27, 1896. It began with the death of the Sultan of Zanzibar and the throne being seized by Khalid bin Barghash. British forces opened fire on the palace from their ships, and just 38 minutes later Barghash surrendered.

YOUR SCORE

Keep a record on a separate sheet of paper of how many answers you got right in each section in the chart below. There are 35 in all. Count one for each question you answer correctly. Then add up your scores to determine your grand total.

Delightful Dinos	
Amazing Ancients	
Heroes and Heroines	
Mad, Bad, and Dangerous to Know	
Would You Believe It?	
TOTAL	

GLOSSARY

aqueduct—A man-made channel, usually in the form of a bridge, built to transport water across long distances.

convicted—To be declared guilty of a crime.

cuneiform—A type of alphabet used in the ancient Middle East that had characters that were wedge- and block-shaped.

evasion—Escaping or avoiding.

extinct—No longer living.

fertile—Able to sustain life.

hieroglyphics—The alphabet used by ancient Egyptians wherein the letters are symbols.

mastermind—A person who plans and directs a complex operation or scheme.

mummification—A form of preservation of bodies in which the moisture from a corpse is removed. This can occur naturally in dry climates or can be done intentionally.

plantation—A large farm or estate on which crops such as coffee, sugar, or rice are grown and are often taken care of by laborors that live there.

protest—An organized demonstration condoning a particular act or policy.

regatta—Boat or yacht race.

Scoville Heat Unit—The measurement of spicy heat of chili peppers.

sultan—The leader of a nation or people in Muslim tradition.

ziggurat—Pyramid built by the Aztecs of South America that looked like a large set of steps.

FURTHER READING

BOOKS

Alexander, Heather, and Meredith Hamilton. *Child's Introduction to the World: Geography, Cultures, and People— From the Grand Canyon to the Great Wall of China*, New York, New York: Black Dog & Leventhal Publishing, 2010.

Boyer, Christopher. *That's Gross!: Icky Facts That Will Test Your Gross-Out Factor*, Washington, D.C.: National Geographic Kids, 2012

Harness, Cheryl. *Ye Olde Weird but True: 300 Outrageous Facts From History*, Washington, D.C.: National Geographic Kids, 2013.

Jennings, Ken. *Ken Jennings' Junior Genius Guides Collection: Maps and Geography; Greek Mythology; U.S. Presidents*, New York, New York: Little Simon, 2015.

Krensky, Stephen, and Rob McClurkan. *The Sweet Story of Hot Chocolate!* (History of Fun Stuff), New York, New York: Simon Spotlight, 2014.

Time for Kids Magazine. *Book of Why: Really Cool People & Places*. New York, New York: Time for Kids, 2014.

Wojtanik, Andrew. *National Geographic Bee Ultimate Fact Book: Countries A to Z. Washington DC*: National Geographic, 2014.

WEBSITES

www.historyforkids.net
A free online source full of fun facts about history!

americanhistory.si.edu/kids/fun-facts-kids
Online source just for kids from the National Museum of
American History at the Smithsonian Institute.

www.coolkidfacts.com
Online source, organized by grade level, that is filled with facts
about history, science, and more!

bbc.co.uk/history/forkids
The British Broadcasting Company's website just for kids.

www.factmonster.com
Great source for fun facts about history, science, and people!

www.kids.nationalgeogrpahic.com
National Geographic's online source for kids, filled with facts,
games, and quizzes!

www.kids-world-travel-guide.com
Online source filled with facts about people and places all over
the globe.

INDEX